102 Tips, Tricks, and Tactics
to be the
Best Executive Assistant

Penney D. Simmons, CAP

ISBN-10: 1983913936
ISBN-13: 9781983913938

Professional Office Plus LLC
1213 Liberty Road
Suite #191
Eldersburg, MD 21784
professionalofficeplus@gmail.com
www.bestexecutiveassistant.com

TABLE OF CONTENTS

INTRODUCTION

My first book, *"101 Ways To Be The Best Executive Assistant,"* written in 2012 was sold all over the world, and I could not be more overjoyed with its success. It has been a great opportunity for me to share my 30 plus years of administrative experience to create a guide for others to become more successful in their careers (and to prevent those new to the field from facing similar challenges and learning some things the hard way, like I did.) It is my hope that this newly expanded and updated version will be even more helpful than the last.

Many books and webinars teach administrative skills, but it is rare to find a resource to teach proper business etiquette and how to maneuver the day-to-day responsibilities that you have to learn on your own while you are actually doing the job. If you are new to the field, this book will give you insight into most of an executive assistant's job duties, and I hope you will find this to be a valuable resource to refer to throughout your career. If you have been in the administrative field for a while, this will be a good refresher, and you might pick up a few new ideas too. Either way, it is my hope that you find this book helpful.

Thank you for sharing my dreams of being a company owner and writer. As you follow your dreams and achieve your goals, I hope you will use this book to become the best you can be.

Penney D. Simmons

Penney D. Simmons, CAP
President & Owner
Professional Office Plus LLC
1213 Liberty Road, Suite #191
Eldersburg, MD 21784
professionalofficeplus@gmail.com
http://www.bestexecutiveassistant.com

102 Tips, Tricks, and Tactics to be the Best EA

The administrative field includes different titles and salary ranges for positions requiring varied skill levels and responsibilities. Executive assistant is referred to most often in this publication, but these 102 tips, tricks, and tactics to be the best executive assistant are useful for anyone in the administrative field. Executive or administrative assistant jobs are the most common titles used today, although there are other jobs, i.e., virtual assistants, secretaries, clerks, office assistants, office managers, coordinators, program assistants, and numerous others that have similar responsibilities.

Being the best you can be in any job gives you a sense of accomplishment and pride. Working in the administrative field can be stressful at times, or depending on your job responsibilities, most of the time, especially when you are working with a demanding boss or team and there are multiple deadlines to meet. Depending on your chosen field and the type of administrative work you do, it is possible that you will be required to work independently with little or no supervision, which requires a great deal of self discipline and good judgment as well as the ability to prioritize, plan, organize, and manage your time.

For those who are new to the administrative field, this book will provide extremely valuable advice to help you get established in your career and prepare you for possible advancement. The following 102 tips, tricks, and tactics will offer a refresher for experienced admins along with some new ideas that might make their life easier. These are in no particular order as they are all equally important.

1. **Be one step ahead of everyone, and anticipate your boss's needs in advance.**

   ✓ Most of the time in administrative jobs, you are expected to take initiative and get things done without being asked. (This may not be the case if you have a boss who likes to sign off on everything before you proceed on projects.)

✓ This may be difficult when you are new to a job, but once you get the hang of things, you will find this is essential. Some examples might include:

- Doing research to help your boss prepare for a meeting or special project

- Setting up audio visual equipment before meetings or making sure the proper requests are submitted so it is done ahead of time

- Ordering supplies such as notebooks, dividers and tabs for handouts

- Making sure there are flip charts and markers in the room and that there is plenty of paper for them to use, if needed.

- Doing things ahead of time to save last minute scrambling and alleviating some of the worries of your boss, so he or she can concentrate on other things that are more important.

- Offering your boss the option of getting their lunch ahead of time or suggesting to have something delivered for all meeting participants, if you know their meetings will go through lunch. (Some assistants are expected to get lunch for their boss on a regular basis depending on how busy their boss is.)

✓ When you and your boss(es) work as a team, it will make it easier to anticipate their needs ahead of time.

✓ Have weekly (or daily) meetings with your boss to stay informed about their priorities and upcoming projects. This will help you with scheduling and prioritizing your workload.

✓ It is important to see the big picture and anticipate the logistics and details that it takes to conduct a successful meeting or plan the perfect event.

✓ Having the ability to anticipate your boss's needs will help you look professional, and most importantly, it will help your boss look prepared and professional as well.

2. **Have self confidence and believe in yourself and your abilities.**

   ✓ Even if you make a mistake, if you make it with confidence, people are more likely to think you are correct (even if you're not). Acknowledge your mistake and learn from it.

   ✓ Confident people get further in their careers than non-confident people, and they are given more opportunities because they appear to be more capable to deal with challenges.

   ✓ If you are harshly criticized for what you feel is for no reason, don't doubt yourself and your abilities, and if you are correct about something, defend yourself.

   ✓ If you lower your self-esteem to someone else's criticism, you always feel defeated and beat down. Don't let this happen to you, and hold your head high and be proud of your accomplishments and skills/abilities.

3. **Anyone can have a high IQ. EA's should have a high EQ too. If you're not familiar with EQ, or EI as it is sometimes referred to, it stands for Emotional Intelligence Quotient. EQ is essential to be successful in business. It is how you control your emotions and reactions, how you interpret other people's emotions, and how you are able to be empathetic to better relate to others.**

✓ If you are interested in learning more about EQ and how it is essential for assistants, I recommend the following:

- Office Dynamics had a guest blogger on April 12, 2017, Brandi Britton, district president for OfficeTeam, writing on *"5 Reasons Why You Need Emotional Intelligence"* (https://officedynamics.com/5-reasons-need-emotional-intelligence)

- Executive Partnership's article *"Emotional Intelligence – Why is it a vital skill for assistants?"* (https://www.executivepartnerships.co.uk/emotional-intelligence-vital-skill-assistant)

- Renee DeVaughn's May 22, 2016 article on *"Understanding Emotional Intelligence"* (http://www.devaughnnarratives.com/understanding-emotional-intelligence)

4. **Always be ethical and keep your moral compass and standards intact. (I am a firm believer that honesty is always the best policy.)**

✓ Several years ago, I attended an IAAP seminar and one of the speakers was **Nan DeMars**, author of the book, *"You've Got To Be Kidding: How to Keep Your Job Without Losing Your Integrity!"* She gave an example in her presentation that I will never forget. It was the quote, *"I will never lie for you, but you also should know I will never lie to you."* Check out her article in the Star Tribune, *"Business Forum: There Is No Cover For Lying To The Boss."* You can find it at the following link: www.startribune.com/business-forum-there-is-no-cover-for-lying-to-the-boss/422145253.

✓ There may be a time when a boss might ask you to be less than truthful to cover for them. Do only what you feel comfortable doing in these types of situations. Keep in mind that there is probably a way to cover for your boss without compromising your ethics and without making your boss look bad in the process.

5. **Always maintain your composure during a crisis and when you are under a lot of stress.**

    ✓ There is a great saying from Gillette's Dry Idea deodorant commercial from the early 1980's, *"Never let them see you sweat."* (You can fall apart later after the crisis is over when nobody is looking.)☺

6. **Don't beat yourself up for mistakes.**

    ✓ Do your best to learn from your mistakes, so they don't happen again.

    ✓ Keep in mind that the higher level of executive your boss is, the more impact your mistakes may have on yourself and others. If you are working for presidents or vice presidents, etc. of a company, your mistakes could have more of an impact because it is more visible and has the potential to affect more people.

7. **Take criticism graciously, and try not to take things too personally.**

    ✓ Consider the criticism to be a productive, learning experience.

    ✓ Pick yourself up, smile, and move forward. There is no need to have a bad attitude or sulk about it, because that will only make things worse.

8. **Push yourself beyond your comfort zone.**

    ✓ By taking a chance and going beyond your comfort zone, you get the opportunity to see and do new things, which can increase your skill level and abilities.

9. Be aware of the small details that impact the big picture.

✓ Keeping the small details in mind goes well beyond scheduling though. Most bosses are visionaries who look at the big picture. In doing so, they may not realize the time and materials it will take to accomplish the administrative tasks for their next project. (That's your expertise!)

✓ You need to let your boss know the timing constraints on ordering materials, making copies, assembling books, etc. Some bosses are not aware of the time it takes to make multiple copies and put handouts together, so you might need to remind them of these things as it could impact their deadline.

✓ Depending on your office, printer/copier availability might also be an issue. For example, if time and money are factors, you should let your boss know that if you have to send a job to a local printer for an overnight turn around, it will be costly.

✓ Sometimes you have to anticipate scheduling conflicts and eliminate them ahead of time.

✓ There will be times when you need to reschedule meetings to avoid double booking.

✓ You might also need to book planning meetings or pre-meetings to get ready for large events or more formal meetings.

10. Timing is everything.

✓ If your boss is having a bad day, it's not the best time to ask for a raise or a vacation day.

✓ Try to gauge what is going on throughout your boss's day and plan accordingly.

✓ It is not a good idea to schedule a dinner meeting on a Friday night or a 7:00 a.m. staff meeting on a Monday.

11. Always help your boss look his or her professional best.

✓ Remember that you are representing the company as well as your boss and yourself, so maintain professionalism at all times.

✓ Make sure you are professional on the phone, in e-mails, and in person, etc.

✓ Be sure to check for spelling and grammar errors. Use caution and be sure to question results as they may not be accurate depending on word usage, context, etc. Also, make sure the formatting and font(s) are consistent on everything.

✓ Keep your boss(es) informed, so they are aware of important things internally and externally that could impact them, your department, or pending projects.

✓ You do not want your boss to appear clueless or uninformed as this also reflects negatively on you.

12. Be a perfectionist, but not to the point that you never get anything accomplished.

✓ For anyone who is a perfectionist, this can be difficult to do. (Trust me, I know firsthand.) ☺ You want everything to be perfect, but there are times when deadlines prevent this from happening. Take this book for an example. If I waited until it was perfect, I would have never gotten it published.

✓ Knowing how to prioritize is a critical part of the job. Make sure you can deliver the essential items needed. Also, keep in mind that sometimes, you have to let some things go in order to meet deadlines. Having something 100% perfect takes time, and you rarely have enough time for that when you are under a deadline.

✓ Although this is extremely difficult for those who are worriers, don't worry or get stressed out about the things that are out of your control. With as difficult as it might be, you need to let everything else that you can't control go. If you don't, you will quadruple your stress level unnecessarily.

✓ Always do the best job you can do with the resources and time you have available.

13. Continue to improve your skills and learn new skills. Take advantage of any classes offered and/or tuition reimbursement opportunities for college degrees.

✓ Refer to the Website Resources section of this book for low cost or free opportunities.

✓ Not only is it important to increase your skill level for your current employer, but it is also important to maintain your self esteem and to continue to expand your resume to attract future employers.

✓ You will also get a good sense of accomplishment from learning new skills, especially if it is something you can use to make your life easier, make you a more valuable contributor, and make your current job go more smoothly.

✓ Some classes provide good networking opportunities to meet others in your field. There are several admin professional organizations that hold office seminars to improve your skills and network. Depending on your work situation, you company might even be willing to pay for your seminar or class fees.

✓ Technology is constantly changing, so you need to keep up with all of the latest trends in software and hardware. It is also important to know how these trends impact your business.

✓ If your employer offers opportunities to get a college degree through tuition reimbursement, take full advantage of this benefit. Keep in mind that some administrative jobs may require a Bachelors degree.

✓ Be sure to pay close attention to the wording if you have to sign an agreement for tuition reimbursement as you might have to stay with the company a certain period of time after your last class is completed to qualify for reimbursement.

✓ As mentioned earlier, learn as much as you can to continually increase your skill level and make yourself more valuable and marketable.

14. Attend seminars and conferences whenever you have the opportunity.

✓ Seminars/webinars are important to expand your knowledge on office trends, administrative skills, and software programs, etc. Even if you pick up one skill or piece of useful information, it will be worth your time.

✓ There is a possibility your company might pay for you to attend, but you will never find out, if you don't ask.

✓ Be on the lookout for free seminars or webinars. I highly recommend the free monthly webinars sponsored by Joan Burge, founder and CEO of Office Dynamics International. Their Website also has great resources, some of which are also free. Their webinar information can be found at: https://officedynamics.com/webinars.

✓ If you work for a large company, check with other admins in your company to see if they would like to attend webinars with you. Maybe your departments could split the cost, or you might get a group discount if enough admins attend.

15. Be early for meetings.

✓ Prepare the room, and when possible, make copies of materials ahead of time.

✓ Make sure that the conference call dial-in numbers are working and/or video conferencing, if applicable.

✓ If a projector and laptop are needed for projecting slides, make sure everything is working properly ahead of time.

✓ Anticipate technical difficulties, and do dry-runs beforehand to try to eliminate any issues the day of the meeting.

✓ Problems will always occur when you least expect them. Be prepared with a work-around, in case you might need it. You may want to have IT support on stand-by to assist, if needed.

✓ Make sure if you ordered food or catering that everything is set up and ready before the meeting starts. Request catering set-up to be done well before the meeting time. Also, make preparations to be sure that hot food stays hot and cold food stays cold. You don't want someone to get sick if a meeting runs over or to have cold food if they don't break for lunch on time.

16. Dress for success.

✓ A good guide is to dress as professionally as your boss does, since you are representing them and your company. If your boss wears a suit, dress accordingly.

✓ If you are seeking upward mobility in your career, the rule of thumb is to dress for the job you want, not the job you have.

✓ If you are on a shoestring budget, buy two or three outfits that coordinate with each other, so you can mix and match the pieces for different looks. For example, a good starter wardrobe would be a blazer, a skirt, pants, a dress, and two or three blouses.

✓ If you are just starting out and cannot afford suits, dress as professionally as possible until your financial situation improves.

✓ If you have a limited budget, another good alternative is to shop for clothes at your local thrift store or consignment shop, such as Goodwill, Salvation Army, etc. You might be able to find business clothes for much less than what you would pay in department stores. Plus, you can feel good knowing you are supporting a charity with your purchase.

✓ Accessories can change the look of the same outfit completely, such as scarves, jewelry, etc. Just remember to be conservative.

✓ If you want to be seen as a professional, try to be as conservative as possible. Maintaining a professional appearance is required when you are representing your boss and the company. Tattoos should be covered, and visible piercings should be limited to your ears. (If you have facial piercings, in your cheek, tongue, nose, eyebrow, lip, or chin, etc., you might want to take them out during work hours.) You want to be remembered for your skills, not your tattoos, Mohawk hairdo, unique hair color, or piercings.☺

✓ Safety should be taken into consideration, because you don't want to risk getting your scarf caught in the paper shredder or getting your favorite ring caught in the copier. Also, you wouldn't want to be wearing open toed shoes in areas where closed toe shoes or steel toe boots are required.☺

17. Stay informed to the best of your ability.

✓ Even if your boss does not share certain information with you, be sure to keep up with trends in your industry as well as local and global current events. These items will help you to support your team better. You appear more knowledgeable and informed when speaking with your bosses and coworkers.

✓ Read the Company newsletter and review the website constantly to ensure you are on top of what the company departments are doing.

18. Read everything you can get your hands on at work.

✓ Read correspondence (e-mail or snail mail), contracts that cross your desk, trade magazines, journals, articles regarding trends in your industry, etc.

✓ If you have access to your boss's e-mail or if you are in charge of their e-mail inbox, read everything you can to stay informed and keep your boss updated as well. Alert them to urgent matters by updating them between meetings.

✓ Check out Free Trade Magazines at http://www.freetrademagazines.com, which offers many white papers and trade publications.

19. **Take classes in your industry and read trade journals or publications to be more informed and to better understand the work your team is doing.**

   ✓ Examples of this would be legal, medical, real estate, etc. I took a medical terminology class when working at a hospital, and it resulted in me getting promoted to a medical secretary. I also took a real estate class to get my license, so I could understand the contracts I was processing while working at a real estate office. (I could not be an active agent, since that would be a conflict of interest. However, I kept my real estate license on referral to obtain a commission for any clients I referred.)

   ✓ Classes are extremely helpful if you plan on moving out of the administrative field and into another role in the industry.

   ✓ Classes to improve your computer skills are extremely important as software changes are happening daily. It is critical to be able to be on top of all the changes as software advances and more programs are added.

   ✓ Ask your boss if the company would be willing to pay for the classes.

20. **Know how to format basic letters, reports, etc.**

   ✓ Some companies have their own brand, style, format, and/or company font, graphics, etc. so be sure to ask about formatting preferences and templates, if you are new to your job.

21. **Be prepared to offer to do administrative tasks for others or hold someone's hand if they need you to.**

   ✓ Although some bosses are knowledgeable about their job, they might not have the skills or know-how to perform certain administrative tasks themselves. (That is why they need you!) For example, they might not know how to make copies, format a document, send interoffice mail, etc. Help other executives, even the ones who are not in your department. This shows you are a team player and are willing to assist others.

22. **When keeping someone else's calendar, leave time between meetings.**

   ✓ If you book meetings too close together and the first morning meeting runs over the scheduled time, there is the potential for your boss to be late to meetings for the rest of the day.

   ✓ Pad meeting schedules because most meetings run over the allotted time.

   ✓ Allow some time for your boss to check e-mails or return phone calls between meetings.

23. **Be diplomatic, especially if you are asked for your opinion.**

   ✓ There are times when being subtle while giving your opinion is better than being blunt.

   ✓ Being diplomatic is so important as we are often tasked with being in delicate situations and circumstances.

   ✓ No matter what the situation is, take a step back and try to remove the emotions from the topic if you are involved.

   ✓ Most importantly, maintain your professionalism at all times.

24. If you have a problem bad enough to take it to your boss, you should also suggest possible solutions.

✓ This will show your boss that you are an independent thinker and are trying to help solve the problem to the best of your ability.

✓ Present the facts (removing your emotions) along with the solutions. Write down your talking points ahead of time to maintain your focus.

✓ Remember most bosses do not have time for long discussions. When you have an opportunity to meet with your boss about these matters, be direct and get to the point quickly.

✓ Don't cry wolf to your boss too many times. If you bring trivial matters to your boss too frequently, when it is something you can resolve yourself, it is possible that your boss will not take you seriously the next time.

✓ If the problem is low priority, it is possible it might resolve itself over time. Most of the time, problems that are low priority in the scheme of things can wait, especially if your boss is dealing with more important matters.

✓ If you interrupt your boss for a low priority problem when he or she is in the middle of a crisis, it is possible that in addition to not getting any help with your problem, you could also ruin your credibility by being insensitive to other urgent issues that are more important.

✓ As mentioned earlier, timing is everything, and this is something you have some control over. If you know your boss is having a bad day, it's probably not a good time to present a problem to them, especially if it can wait until later.

25. Be a team player and help out wherever you can.

✓ This will help you by learning new skills and increasing your experience with certain tasks.

✓ It will provide you with an opportunity to learn what other departments do and expand your knowledge of your company. It will also give you exposure to people who you might not have been able to work with otherwise.

✓ This can be a great opportunity to network with others, if you are working with a team on a project.

26. Keep confidential information confidential.

✓ Some jobs allow you the opportunity to see confidential information that cannot be shared. You cannot breach this trust by sharing the information with others. If you do, it could cost you your job.

✓ Your boss will not trust you with confidential information, if they suspect you are sharing it with others.

✓ Some companies require you to sign a confidentiality agreement stating that you will not disclose their business secrets.

27. Stay out of the rumor mill and do not encourage gossip.

✓ In addition to looking unprofessional, if you gossip, you stand the chance of destroying the trust between you and your boss as well as other coworkers.
✓ There are some coworkers who will try to persuade you to share confidential information that has been entrusted to you. Do not get drawn into this as it could ruin your reputation and possibly cost you your job.

28. **Accentuate your skills and expertise, and whenever possible take advantage of opportunities to do what you do best.**

   ✓ Remember to make your talents known, because if you don't toot your own horn, nobody else will.

29. **Make it easy on yourself, use templates, create your own, borrow from other admins, or search online.**

   ✓ Don't start from scratch on something unless you absolutely have to. Using templates that are readily available can save a lot of time.

30. **If you need help with something, ask for help.**

   ✓ Don't waste time struggling with a project, especially when someone might be able to help you learn how to get the job done in half the time and save you unnecessary steps.

   ✓ You will be more productive and efficient by spending your time more wisely and asking for help when you need it.

   ✓ If you are not totally sure what your boss wants, show your boss your initial work before you are finished with a project. This will prevent you from wasting time doing the whole project over if it is not what is expected.

   ✓ Asking questions can also help improve the accuracy and quality of your work. If you don't understand something, you might do it incorrectly.

31. **Ask questions if you are unsure or are not familiar with certain terms or acronyms.**

   ✓ If you are new to the field, or if your co-workers are in a technical field, ask for the definition of terms or acronyms, if you don't understand something

✓ Ask if there is a list of company acronyms or buzz words. If not, make your own.

32. Get a mentor and/or be a mentor to help someone else.

✓ You will learn valuable information from your mentor, and they can be a good sounding board.

✓ A mentor and/or an accountability partner helps keep you on track with your professional or personal projects or goals.

✓ Becoming a mentor to a new hire can provide you with fresh ideas as you can also learn from their experiences too. They may have skills that you do not have, and you can learn from each other.

33. If you don't already have one, get your own personal Board of Advisors.

✓ These are people who give you career advice, offer you suggestions, and guide you towards a successful career or business, if you are a virtual assistant or self-employed.

✓ I recently heard a quote that said if you're the smartest person in the room, then you're in the wrong room. The following article explains why:

- Matthew Turndog Turner's article, *"Why Being the Smartest Person In The Room Is The Dumbest Thing You Can Be"* states this well by saying, "The smartest person in the room is the only one in it incapable of learning." (You can find it at Medium.com at http://bit.ly/2GJ3Ze8.)

✓ Surround yourself with people who will keep you on your toes and challenge you to push yourself and reach for the stars.

34. Consider joining administrative and/or professional organizations and network with others.

✓ There are opportunities to improve your skills through obtaining a certification or attending classes and conferences.

✓ The people you meet will be good resources, and you could also make life-long friends.

✓ Learn from fellow members in other industries and get advice or ideas on problem solving and working more efficiently.

✓ There are numerous professional organizations you can join. You need to find out which one(s) are the best for you and your career goals. Some examples:
  - International Association of Administrative Professionals (IAAP) – http://www.iaap-hq.org

  - American Society of Administrative Professionals (ASAP) – http://www.asaporg.com

  - Association of Executive and Administrative Professionals (AEAP) – http://www.theaeap.com

  - LinkedIn is a good professional Website for networking, and it also offers groups and associations you can join.

35. Help new employees get acclimated, and treat them the way you would want to be treated if you were new.

✓ Do what you can to get everything ready for the new person's arrival, i.e. order supplies, order their laptop and/or cell phone, have their office cleaned and set up ahead of time, etc.

✓ You could create a book with helpful information on your company and department with important policies, branding info, organizational charts, travel info, etc. It is helpful to have all of the information in one place, and new employees find this type of information extremely helpful.

36. Have a good rapport with everyone.

✓ Do your best to be cordial with everyone. Even if you might not like someone as a person, try to maintain a professional working relationship with them.

✓ Most importantly, don't burn bridges with anyone. You never know when you might have to work with them again. If you are with a company for several years, there is a possibility you might have to work with a new boss or new team at some point, especially if you decide to change jobs and/or departments at your current company.

37. When possible, do what you enjoy doing.

✓ If you cannot do what you love at work, do something on your own time, such as getting a hobby, which satisfies your creative side, etc. In addition to writing, I enjoy painting, crocheting, and make jewelry, which gives me a creative outlet that I don't have at work. These are great stress relievers.☺

38. Don't bring your personal life to work.

✓ Sometimes, personal matters follow you to work whether you want them to or not, but do your best to keep your personal life separate from work.

✓ It is important that you maintain your concentration to do your job well and stay focused to insure you maintain high work quality and stay safe by avoiding accidents on the job.

✓ Limit your personal phone calls and e-mail communications while at work.

39. Proof read before sending anything out or hitting send, even if you are under a strict deadline.

✓ Whenever possible, have someone else proof important assignments for you.

✓ If you cannot have someone else proof your work, step away from your project for a while to get a fresh perspective. (Sometimes you read what you want it to say instead of seeing what is actually on the page.)

✓ Read what you have written out loud. This will often assist in making sure it says what you want to convey.

40. Don't send e-mails or post anything online that you wouldn't want your boss, other coworkers, or your friends or family to see because something could come back to haunt you.

✓ This will save you a lot of potential embarrassment if you state something incorrectly or if you say something inappropriate.

✓ If you post something controversial, vulgar, obscene, or inflammatory, etc., it could cost you your job.

✓ Remember that anything you do on company time becomes part of their permanent records, so don't use work e-mail for personal use. Also, don't check your personal e-mail account on your work computer.

✓ If you are angry or upset about something, save the e-mail and come back to it, or have a close friend/co-worker check the content and tone of the e-mail before you send it. Try to take the emotions out of your response and stay calm, so you can maintain your professionalism.

✓ Sleep on it. Tomorrow could change your outlook on the situation.

✓ Don't use "Reply All" (unless you really need to).

41. Double check e-mail addresses before sending e-mails.

✓ There are people who have similar names, and you could accidentally send e-mails to someone you didn't intend them to go to if you don't double check the address.

✓ If you are using an auto fill feature or program, be sure to double check e-mail addresses and information on completed forms to make sure they are correct.

42. Keep your phone or a pen and paper handy, when you are away from your desk.

✓ If you are stopped in the hallway with a request you want to remember it when you return.

✓ If you get interrupted or side tracked, there is a possibility you might forget something.

✓ Take a pen and paper to your boss's office and/or meetings to write down instructions, action items, and notes.

43. Use what works best for you to keep track of your "to-do" list and leave yourself reminders.

✓ Place reminders on your calendar to keep track of deadlines (use a program such as Outlook, a paper calendar, or both).

✓ Assign yourself tasks in Outlook and check them off as you accomplish them.

✓ Write sticky notes (electronically on your desktop in Windows or using pen and paper).

✓ Keep a tickler file, so you can keep track of important reminders or deadlines as you check it each day. (A tickler file is an accordion folder with slots 1 through 31 for each day of the month, and there is also a slot for each month.)

✓ Sending e-mails to yourself with follow-up deadlines is also helpful.

✓ Keep a running paper "to-do" list on your desk on a note pad and cross things off or put a checkmark by them as each item is completed. This will provide a good record of what you have accomplished.

✓ Go over the list at the end of each day, so you can add any new projects and be ready for the next morning.

44. **If you have a long "To Do" list, after taking deadlines and priorities into consideration, tackle the small tasks first, so your assignments won't seem so overwhelming.**

✓ This will give you a sense of accomplishment and ease the stress level for you early in the day.

45. **Be the "go to" person for everything.**

✓ Make yourself a valuable asset to the company by being a helpful resource, whether it is as simple as assisting with finding office supplies or knowing who to call to get something accomplished.

✓ You don't need to know how to do everything, but you can point someone in the right direction or direct them to someone else who knows. Follow through to assist them when possible.

46. Go the extra step or extra mile.

✓ Most bosses and coworkers will appreciate your efforts.

✓ If you go the extra mile to be more thorough, it will have a positive reflection on your work ethic, and it could save you more time in the long run.

47. YouTube and Google are great "How To" resources, if you need to learn something.

✓ It's free! There are usually several videos to choose from on the same topics. If you don't like the first one you find, choose another one.

✓ You might have to research your topic on your own time, if these sites are restricted or blocked at your work.

48. Make yourself invaluable.

✓ Demonstrate how you "add value" to the company.

✓ If you can fill a particular niche that no one else can, make sure others know how valuable your unique skills are.

49. Help save the company money.

✓ Find ways to help contribute to the bottom line by either saving money or generating revenue in some way.

✓ Offer suggestions on ways to save money such as less expensive office supplies that are comparable to what the company is currently using.

✓ Take an active role by creating or joining sub-committees and task forces to find ways to save money on expenses.

50. Take advantage of free resources available to you online.

✓ If you are a Virtual Assistant or own your own business, this can be extremely helpful.

✓ Some examples include free PowerPoint templates and free Microsoft classes on Microsoft.com.

51. Don't surf the Web or play games at work.

✓ Some companies monitor your online activities closely.

✓ Using company time for Web surfing, downloading personal information, watching videos, etc. could cost you your job.

✓ Sometimes certain Internet activities drain company resources, i.e. Internet speed and bandwidth.

52. Put on a happy face, no matter what challenges are ahead of you.

✓ Your job will be easier if everyone finds you friendly and approachable, even during stressful times when you are under a great deal of pressure.

53. Be optimistic!

✓ Have a glass half full kind of attitude or completely full if you can manage it. ☺

54. If you have to make an executive decision, weigh all of the possible outcomes carefully before deciding.

✓ Be sure to get as much information as possible and make sure you have all of the facts.

✓ Look at the big picture, and try to judge how your decision might impact the situation or outcome.

✓ Get a second opinion from a co-worker or fellow admin, if possible to help you make your decision. (But, don't throw them under the bus if things go wrong.)

55. Keep your options open and be open to new opportunities.

✓ Be on the lookout for opportunities both inside and outside your current company. You never know when the next great opportunity might come along.

✓ Keep your resume up to date. Be sure to include additional education as you complete it and added job responsibilities.

56. Whether you decide to make being an Executive Assistant your career or reach for the stars, be the best you can be.

✓ Plan your career path carefully. There is a possibility that you can be pigeon-holed or stuck in the administrative field, if you don't have a well thought out career plan for advancement.

✓ Make sure you continue to maintain marketable skills in case you lose your job or decide to take a new job either inside your current company or with a new organization. Keep your skill level current with technology advancements.

✓ If you want to move to another field other than administrative, be sure to investigate the salary range, required skills, and training required, so you can prepare accordingly.

57. Make suggestions on how the company could be more efficient.

✓ Suggest ways to improve the way things are done.

✓ Keep in mind the old saying that time is money.

✓ Just because something has always been done a certain way doesn't mean it has to continue being done that way, especially if it is either a time waster or process that is no longer needed or obsolete.

58. In addition to keeping your resume up-to-date, create a bio for yourself, a portfolio of your work, and as an added bonus, get your own personal Website.

✓ It doesn't cost much to get a Website with your name. I keep my contact information at **http://www.PenneySimmons.com**. It's easy to do through popular sites that sell domain names if your name is available, and some companies even let you set up one page for free without monthly hosting charges. It's impressive to future employers and a good way for friends to keep in touch with you. However, keep in mind that there are "bots" on the Web trolling for phone numbers and e-mail addresses, so putting information out to the public also has its downsides as well.

✓ You never know when you might need a bio or resume for networking purposes, college classes, new job opportunities with other companies, your current employer, or for when you write your best seller. ☺

www.bestexecutiveassistant.com

✓ Memorizing your bio will help you when networking with others. You will appear more professional by getting the important information about yourself across in five minutes or less. (This is usually referred to as an "elevator speech.")

✓ Keeping a portfolio of your work is great to take on interviews or for virtual assistants to use to show to potential clients. (Virtual assistants can also include this information on their Website too.) Show off examples of presentations you have done, Websites you created, your best masterpieces to get the job or client of your dreams.

59. When buying supplies, purchase only what is needed at the time.

✓ Avoid storing too many excess supplies as it costs the company by tying up resources.

✓ Anticipate the need for supplies that are most often requested by your boss and other team members, and order accordingly.

✓ If you are preparing for a regularly scheduled meeting or conference, be sure to have everything on hand ahead of time, so you are not scrambling at the last minute.

60. Consider keeping a paper calendar with a monthly view. It's the best way to see both your business and personal schedules at a glance.

✓ Even if you use an iPhone or Smart Phone with Google, Outlook, or another automated scheduling program, it's helpful to have a monthly view at a glance for planning purposes. (Be prepared in case your battery dies or you can't get to your phone or computer for some reason.)

✓ In addition to my Outlook calendar, I keep a month-at-a-glance paper calendar that I always carry with me. It

32

shows me the big picture when planning or scheduling personal and professional appointments. (See #83 on page 40 for information on my *"All-in-One Diary, Datebook, and Dossier..."*)

✓ If your company has a corporate calendar which includes all important meetings, be sure you include these meetings on your calendar to prevent scheduling conflicts.

61. Make a travel folder for each trip your boss takes.

✓ It is extremely helpful for your boss to have his or her travel itinerary, ground transportation information, hotel information, as well as all of the details about the meeting or seminar, etc. all in one place.

✓ Include an envelope to collect receipts. It will make things easier for doing expense reports.

✓ I use colored plastic poly folders which are waterproof, thin, and they travel well. If you have several bosses, you can use a different color for each boss.

✓ Make sure their passport and visa information is up-to-date, and apply for visas well in advance of travel.

✓ If your boss has never traveled to the location, include cultural information, if applicable, hotel fact sheet, nearby restaurants and attractions, etc. Printing out a weather forecast for the duration of their trip is also helpful.

62. Have a great relationship with the receptionist(s) and mailroom.

✓ The people in these positions rarely get enough recognition for their difficult jobs, and they are the most important people in any business.

✓ You never know when you might need to call on them for assistance.

63. Have a great relationship with the audio/visual and other teams you depend on daily.

✓ Since you will be working with several departments on a regular basis, it is important to maintain great relationships with everyone. A little kindness and a positive attitude go a long way.

✓ The audio/visual team and IT are critical to your success at meetings and providing technical support for your boss. Building a positive relationship with these groups is essential.

64. Have a personal life.

✓ Do your best to maintain a good work/life balance.

✓ As mentioned earlier, you should not bring your personal life to work, and the reverse is also true. Leave your work at work when possible.

65. Create a small handbook, so the person who backs you up can cover for you when you are out.

✓ Be sure to keep these instructions readily available, so your backup can easily assist your team in your absence.

66. Keep electronic files well organized with an easy to understand, dependable system.

✓ Be sure to provide instructions for the person who fills in for you when you are on vacation or in case of emergencies.

67. If you keep paper files, keep them well organized and easy to find.

✓ Make sure your boss or backup can easily find what they need in your absence.

68. Take good care of yourself and do your best to stay healthy.

✓ It is important that you take good care of yourself, so you can take care of others both in your personal life and professionally.

✓ If your company offers programs promoting good health, such as gym memberships or diet programs, consider taking advantage of the opportunities being offered.

69. Get a good night's sleep each night to help you stay focused the next day.

✓ Although this is difficult for some people, do your best to get enough rest and take care of yourself. If you don't take good care of yourself, it's difficult to take care of others. ☺

70. Eat breakfast or bring it in with you to eat later.

✓ Breakfast is the most important meal of the day, and you need more than coffee to sustain you throughout the day.

71. Take mini-breaks to stretch and give your eyes and neck a break.

✓ This will give you a fresh look at things and help with proofreading. You will be more productive in the long run. Your body will thank you for the reprieve.

72. Get those steps in!

✓ Be kind to yourself and your body by getting up and moving around occasionally. Stretch your legs from time to time and give your eyes a break from the computer screen.

✓ Consider setting your own personal goals, even if your employer doesn't require it, so you are not stuck at your desk all day.

✓ Some employers require workers to wear a watch that tracks their level of physical fitness, and in some cases, it is tied to their insurance premiums or bonuses.

73. Make sure your desk and computer are set up ergonomically correct, and consider getting a stand-up/adjustable desk.

✓ Be safe and prevent permanent injuries.

✓ I recently got an adjustable desk, so I can stand and work when I want to. When I feel like sitting, I simply lower my desk. It's great to have the option to choose between the two.

74. Try to take a lunch break, and when you do, be sure to take lunch away from your desk.

✓ You will be more productive and refreshed after taking a break away from your desk (even if it is only for a few minutes).

✓ If you stay and eat lunch at your desk, it is possible that you might not get a break. If people see you there, they will assume they can still ask you for assistance.

75. If your boss is open to suggestions, offer them.

✓ Ideas that will save the company time and/or money or suggestions regarding a more efficient way to do things are usually greatly appreciated.

76. Keep important and frequently used resources handy. (Like this book!) ☺

✓ Keep a list of helpful Websites handy and/or bookmark sites in your Favorites.

✓ Make shortcut icons on your desktop for programs and Websites you use most often. (Also, offer to do the same for your boss(es) to save them time as well.)

77. Don't forget to back up your computer in case of viruses, cyber attacks, or a hard drive crash, etc. If you own your own business, have a disaster recovery plan.

✓ With all of the natural disasters we have had world-wide lately, it is important to have a disaster recovery plan. (See Website Resources for a great template and guide.)

✓ Keep in mind that losing a few days of work is better than starting years of work over from scratch.

✓ If you are a virtual assistant or if you own your own small business, the loss of both business and customer information can be financially devastating and time consuming for your business.

✓ Consider getting an external hard-drive in addition to whatever system is backed-up on your company's network. Make sure you know what the company policy is on keeping backup copies and know how to backup your pc.

78. **Plan vacations and sick leave around important meetings and seminars.**

   ✓ If there is someone who backs you up when you are out, make sure that person is available on the days you want to be out, **before** you ask your boss for leave.

   ✓ Depending on the circumstances, there is a possibility your request for leave could be denied, if you request time off during a busy time of the year.

79. **Ask all of the necessary questions for meeting scheduling, and get as many details as possible for event planning.**

   ✓ See Website Resources section of this book for important meeting planning Websites and checklists.

   ✓ Be sure to ask the Who, What, Where, When, and Why, and How long at your first opportunity, so you have all the information you need to start scheduling.

   ✓ Be sure to ask about the number of attendees, theme or occasion, budget for the event, the preferred location(s), room setup (classroom style, board meeting, u-shaped, etc.), catering and meals needed, audio/visual needs, etc.

80. **Know company travel and expense policies and procedures as well as travel restrictions, if you book travel for others or purchase items for the company.**

   ✓ Some travel discounts for large companies are based on the volume or the amount booked with certain vendors. It is important to stick to these policies, so the company continues to receive these discounts.

   ✓ This is especially important if you need to complete expense reports too. Sometimes only certain expenses are reimbursed or you have to use only company approved vendors. Keep on top of the most recent version of the policies to make sure you or your boss do not purchase something that will not be reimbursed by the company.

81. Prioritize assignments.

✓ Make sure you have a deadline for all projects, so you can prioritize accordingly and set up timelines, etc.

✓ If you have more than one boss and there are conflicts, ask your bosses which project should take priority, if you are not sure which one is more important.

82. Try to anticipate last minute projects and deadlines.

✓ Start sending reminders early and often for pre-planned deadlines for projects that are monthly, quarterly, or annually, etc.

✓ Sending frequent reminders is especially helpful to nudge those who tend to wait until the last minute or procrastinate.

✓ These reminders are critical to allow you time to wrap up the remaining steps of the projects, such as printing, and get everything finished on time.

✓ This will help keep your team on track and prevent every project deadline from becoming an emergency.

✓ Try to complete the project in enough time to allow time for your boss to review your work. Be sure to allow time for making edits.

83. Keep an idea book and/or journal for both work and personal use.

✓ Not only is this useful to keep track of great ideas, but a journal can also be therapeutic. However, just be sure to keep anything private and confidential under lock and key and away from prying eyes (at home and at work depending on your individual situation.)

✓ I had a difficult time finding everything in one place, so I created an *"All-in-One Diary, Datebook, and Dossier: Undated Month & Weekly Planner, Medical History Daily Medical Journal & Food Diary, Goal Tracker Gratitude Journal, Lists, and More."* You can find it on Amazon.com, if you think it might fit your needs. I placed monthly index tabs on mine to make it easier to locate things.

84. Do as much work as you can ahead of time.

✓ If you have to create a monthly report in PowerPoint, start getting the template or draft together for the next meeting as soon as the current meeting is finished.

85. Allow time for printing, binding, etc. after presentations are complete.

✓ It is also important to allow for shipping time, if you meeting or conference is off site.

✓ Remind your boss how long it takes to make these types of materials or books, because most bosses don't realize how time consuming this process can be, especially if your copier is unreliable or not readily available because it is shared with other departments. ☺

86. If you have another job or go to school, don't take outside work or homework to your full-time job.

✓ If you surf the Web to do non-work related research, or if you do personal work on company time, you could end up losing your job if you get caught.

87. Make up a folder or book with hard copies for your boss for seminars and new events with details about sessions, attendees, directions, travel info, etc.

- ✓ If they have to fly to their destination, they can review the information on the plane, so they will be prepared when they land. (Also, send them the electronic version of the same documents.)

88. Don't drink too much at company functions.

- ✓ Besides the fact that you might be fired for acting inappropriately at a work function, you don't want to portray yourself as unprofessional.

- ✓ You might say or do things under the influence that you will regret later.

- ✓ Getting home safely after the function is also a concern, so don't drink if you are driving.

89. If you take meeting minutes, be brief but thorough.

- ✓ If you have never attended the meeting before, ask to see a copy of the minutes from the last meeting, so you can get an idea of the type of meeting, general topics of discussion, etc. as well was the style or format of the minutes.

- ✓ Complete the minutes as soon as possible while the meeting is fresh in your mind. This will help insure accuracy. (If possible, record the meeting, so you can refer back to it later for clarification on your notes.)

90. Be loyal to your boss and your company.

- ✓ Even if you are unhappy with your current work situation, threatening to quit, gossiping, and showing signs of not being loyal to your company and boss(es) make you look untrustworthy and it could get you fired.

91. Make a "Mom Kit" or box of supplies, mints, first aid, etc. for seminar attendees.

✓ Anticipate your potential needs as well those of the attendees and create the "Mom Kit" accordingly. (See checklist in back of book on page 73 for more suggestions.)

✓ These types of items are helpful to keep at a show booth or at the check-in/greeting table at a large meeting or conference.

92. Give 100% and always put forth your best effort.

✓ Doing the best you can do is all you can do. You can feel good at the end of the day knowing you have given your best effort.

93. If a caller is transferred to you and you do not have the answers they need, do your best to connect them with a live person who can help, or offer to have someone call them back as soon as possible.

✓ Nothing is more frustrating than to be transferred all around a company's voicemail or in a circle of automated responses. Try to do what you can to help the person obtain the information they need.

94. Most importantly, stay flexible and go with the flow.

✓ Every day is likely to be unpredictable, so roll with the punches.

✓ If you support a team, keep in mind that sometimes each team member has a different priority, so you will need to adjust accordingly.

✓ It is not easy to accept change, but the more you accept it, the less stress and fewer problems you will have.

95. **"Other duties as assigned" is on almost every job description. Do your best to accommodate all requests when possible, even the ones that seem weird or somewhat unreasonable.**

✓ Be willing to do things that are not part of your normal responsibilities.

✓ These assignments might lead you to new opportunities or potential career advancement.

✓ If not, remember they are good character building experiences, something you can add to your resume, or to tell a funny story later.

96. **Don't <u>assume</u> anything. (As the saying goes… It makes an ASS out of U and ME.)**

✓ Making wrong assumptions can lead to major mistakes and misunderstandings.

✓ Verify the facts before making assumptions, jumping to conclusions, or making decisions on partial information.

✓ You don't want to finish the whole project the wrong way and have to start over from scratch or report incorrect or incomplete information.

97. Open communication with your boss and your team is essential.

✓ It is essential to schedule regular meetings with your boss to stay up to date with the status of current projects and keep the lines of communication open.

✓ Make sure your boss knows what your workload is like, the projects you are working on, and who you are working with on a regular basis.

✓ This is a great opportunity to share the projects you are working on for other team members with your boss. Your boss might be so busy that he or she does not know about all of the work you are doing for others as mentioned above.

98. Get involved and engaged.

✓ Engaged and involved are major buzz words in business these days. Participate in your company's employee activities and the activities of your division or department when possible. Examples of these activities are: company health fairs, social committee, etc.

✓ When possible, participate in volunteer opportunities and committees that are of interest to you. It will help build better camaraderie with your co-workers and team members. This will also enable you to establish stronger bonds with the community and other co-workers within your company.

99. Know your company's vision, mission, and goals.

✓ It is important to know your company's goals and what their plans are for the future. Most importantly, you need to know where your job fits into the scheme of things and what you can do to help the company achieve those goals.

100. Each company has its own unique culture as well as different opinions on the importance of admins.

✓ It is possible that you might find yourself in a company that considers admins as a valuable part of the team. In this case, your opinion matters, you are allowed to give input, contribute to projects, participate regularly in meetings, and be and active/participating member of the team.

✓ There is also a possibility that at some point in your career, you might have to work for a company that considers admins to be "non-professionals" literally and figuratively. In this case, admins are not valued, neither is their opinions or input, and they are only allowed to participate in the administrative and logistics aspects of projects as needed. Although it might be difficult, don't let negative thoughts and opinions of admins affect the quality of your work.

101. Don't lose sight of the fact that your administrative skills are an essential part of any business.

✓ When I was taking office technology classes in high school in order to become what was referred to as a "secretary" at that time, I had a teacher who told me that as long as I knew how to type, I could put food on the table. Although typing speed may not be as important as it once was due to advancements in technology, my teacher made a good point. No matter what changes I have gone through in my career with technology advancements or changing companies, I have always been able to find some kind of temporary or permanent form of employment using my administrative skills.

✓ Even though administrative skills are essential, often these positions are reduced or eliminated when companies need to cut back on spending. If you are laid off, the suggestions in this book, such as networking, training classes, updating your resume, and creating a bio, etc. will all be extremely beneficial when trying to find a new job or if you are in search of a better job. LinkedIn is an excellent place to start.

✓ If you find your dream job, but you don't have all of the required skills, ask another admin for help, check YouTube for how-to videos, or go to a class to learn how to do it. If you don't have enough time to learn the required skills for a current opening, you will be prepared for the next time a similar position becomes available.

102. **Use technology to your advantage, and do your best to keep up with all the advances and changes. There are so many apps, Websites and artificial intelligence (AI) and voice user interface (VUI) options available to help make your job and your personal life a little easier.**

✓ Please refer to the next section on Website Resources for additional suggestions/info.

✓ The top six apps that I would recommend trying are as follows:

1. **IFTTT** stands for *"If This Then That"* and it is AWESOME! This app allows hundreds of apps and devices to work together. You can control all kinds of things with this app by enabling applets. It makes suggestions to get you started. You can even control things by voice if you turn on applets that use Amazon Alexa or Google Assistant. Check out their Website to learn more at https://ifttt.com.

2. **Open Office** – This has both free and paid versions. It is compatible with Microsoft office products. The 'pro' version is sometimes available for a free trial period. You can check out their Website for more

info at
https://www.openoffice.org/product/index.html.

3. **Evernote** – Referred to in the Website Resources section on page 55. You can download the app or go to their Website for more information at https://evernote.com.

4. **Waze** – I enjoy this better than Google Maps. "Wazers" [drivers] share traffic information with each other via the app to save commute time and find the fastest way to get to their destination. (https://www.waze.com)

5. **Dropbox** – Allows you to store files and access them from your phone or pc. You can also share files with others. This is great for large presentations. (https://www.dropbox.com/register)

6. **Any.do** includes to-do lists, a calendar, reminders, and a planner. You can sign up with Google, Facebook, or email. The premium version charges a small monthly fee. (https://www.any.do)

✓ There are too many apps to mention here, and new ones seem to come out all the time. I recommend reviewing several articles and/or books to find which ones would be the most beneficial to you.

- Several years ago, I attended a Webinar that **Beth Ziesenis** presented on helpful apps and tech tools. I also have her books. Her Website is https://yournerdybestfriend.com Three of her books that you might find helpful are:

  o *"The Big Book of Apps: Your Nerdy BFF's Guide to (Almost) Every App in the Universe"* o *"Release Your Inner Nerd: Apps, Tech Tools, and Tips To Get Organized, Get Creative, and Get Ahead"*

o *"Nerd Know-How: The 27+ Best Apps for Work... & How to Use 'Em!"*

- **Tom's Guide.com** offers an article on *"Best Productivity Apps"* of 2018 by John Corpuz and Jackie Dove, which can be found at the following link: https://www.tomsguide.com/us/pictures-story/588-best-productivity-apps.html#s21.

- **InsideHook.com** offers *"The 21 Best Productivity Apps: or How to Save 90 Minutes Per day"* by Kirk Miller at the following link: https://www.insidehook.com/nation/the-21-best-productivity-apps-for-2018.

- **PC Magazine.com** has an article on *"The Best Productivity Apps of 2018"* by Jill Duffy, which is broken down into different categories and lists which ones are free and for purchase at the following link: https://www.pcmag.com/article2/0,2817,2395938,00.asp.

- **PC Magazine's** *"10 Must-Have Android Apps of 2017"* (https://www.pcmag.com/article2/0,2817,2374865,00.asp)

- **Medium.com** has an article on *"25 Productivity Apps to Explore in 2018"* by Francesco D'Alessio, which can be found at: https://medium.com/the-mission/25-productivity-apps-to-explore-in-2018-dc4a3fb9a8a2.

- **Workzone.com** has an article by Copely Sutton on *"The 25 Best Productivity Apps To Help You Do More In Less Time."* It can be found at the following link: https://www.workzone.com/blog/best-productivity-apps.

✓ Artificial Intelligence (AI) or Virtual User Interface (VUI), i.e. Siri, Cortana, Alexa, Google Home, etc. can take over basic administrative tasks like meeting scheduling, shopping, arranging an Uber, ordering pizza, etc. I have Alexa at home. It is great for reminders, alarms, playing music, and asking some basic questions. I have not been brave enough to enable the voice shopping or have it run my calendar yet. I have also learned that you need be specific with the questions to ask in order to get it to do exactly what you want.

- **TomsGuide.com** has an article on, *"50 Best Amazon Alexa Skills"* (http://bit.ly/2otd6c0)

- *"How To Harness AI To Improve Workplace Efficiency"* by **Information-Age.com** can be found at the following link: http://www.information-age.com/harness-ai-improve-workplace-efficiency-123469118.

- *"Everything You Need To Know About AI Assistants, From Siri to Ozlo"* is a helpful article on the **Fast Company** Website at the following link: https://www.fastcompany.com/3059719/handicapping-the-ai-assistants-from-siri-to-ozlo.

- A recent article, *"AI can take over our mundane tasks. Here's how human workers can learn new, more stimulating skills"* by Gordon Ritter is also worth reading. It can be found on the **Recode.net** Website on check it out at: https://www.recode.net/2017/10/18/16492156/coaching-cloud-future-work-jobs-artificial-intelligence-ai-enterprise-employee-training.

These 102 tips, tricks, and tactics to be the best executive assistant provides a good foundation for you to build on in your career or a great refresher, if you have been in the administrative field for a while. Of course, this is not an exhaustive list, but it's a good place to start. Remember that you can do anything that you set your mind to, and if you give 100% and have the desire to succeed, you will be the best executive assistant you can be.

For more information and additional resources, check out my Website at **http://www.bestexecutiveassistant.com**.

Website Resources

The majority of these Websites offer free or low cost content. The URL addresses are listed, so those reading the print version of this book can type the addresses into their browser. Note that some of the really long Website addresses have been condensed and abbreviated using **https://bitly.com.** If you find any of the Website links to be inactive or inaccurate, please let me know, and I will change or remove them from future versions of this book.

AllMyFaves.com lists various Websites under different categories. Keep this as your homepage to have a lot of options readily available.

Meeting Planning

These Websites include time converters for global meetings as well as helpful checklists to make sure you have everything you need.

✓ **Marriott Meeting Calculators & Checklists** – I recommend starting with this site first as it contains almost everything you need for planning both professional and personal events. It includes links to pdf checklists for a planning timeline, site inspection and selection, budgeting, event promotion, negotiating, and catering. (http://www.marriott.com/meeting-event-hotels/event-planning-checklist.mi)

✓ **Harvard Business Review** (HBR.org) – *"A Checklist for Planning Your Next Big Meeting,"* which can be found at: (https://hbr.org/2015/03/a-checklist-for-planning-your-next-big-meeting) Also, HBR's "Tools You Need to Make Every Meeting More Productive." This article has a lot of good suggestions on apps you can use to be more productive (https://hbr.org/2015/03/the-tools-you-need-to-make-every-meeting-more-productive)

✓ **Meeting Planning Resources.org** – Meeting planning Websites by location as well as articles

✓ **SuccessfulMeetings.com** and **MeetingsNet.com** – Both sites contain articles and news on meeting planning and trends for all types of meetings. I also subscribe to several of their newsletters.

✓ **KeyNoteResource.com** – Provides links to corporate several different types of event planner service providers, i.e. audio visual, registration, etc. (https://www.keynoteresource.com/CorporateEventPlanningLinks.html)

✓ **TheBalance.com** has several great articles:

  - *"Don't Overlook the Importance of An Event Planning Checklist"* – (https://www.thebalance.com/why-you-need-an-event-planning-checklist-4017891)

  - Free basic event planning checklist in Excel – (http://eventplanningblueprint.com/free-eventplanning-checklist-event-managers)

  - *"The Complete Guide To Event Budgeting"* – (https://www.thebalance.com/the-complete-guide-to-event-budgeting-1223678)

  - *"Meeting Planning – Organizing Conventions and Conferences"* (http://bit.ly/2F4Vkp2)

✓ **MeetingsToday.com** – Meeting/Event Planning Checklists – (https://www.meetingstoday.com/Resource-Center/Meeting-Event-Planning-Checklists)

✓ **World Time Server.com** – Global Time Converter for Meeting Planning (https://www.worldtimeserver.com/meeting-planner.aspx)

✓ **World Time Buddy.com** – Time zone converter and meeting planning tool. Offers up to four locations free. Monthly memberships for purchase allow you to add additional locations.

Templates, Labels, Dividers, & More

Templates save time, and they also provide you with new ideas and fresh perspectives. Be sure to read the fine print when something is advertised as free as some Websites require additional charges. If you are unable to download the template, make sure you do not find yourself in a situation where your finished project is essentially held hostage until you pay money to have it released. Also, use caution when downloading anything online as it could have a virus. Doing so is at your own risk, and some companies have fire walls that prevent you from downloading items or installing software.

- ✓ **Microsoft.com** – Free templates by category, event and occasion, or by app: Word, Excel, PowerPoint (https://templates.office.com) See next section on Free Software for additional Microsoft compatible templates from OpenOffice.

- ✓ **Avery.com** (Avery Dennison) – Free templates and software, step-by-step guides, design and print online, plus more. I use this site often for labels and index tabs.

- ✓ **Top-Products** – Free templates for binder covers, indexes, and PowerPoint, this includes templates for brands like Pendaflex, Cardinal, and more. (http://easycoversandmore.com/topsproducts/easycovers/index.html)

- ✓ **Worldlabel.com** – Offers label templates by material and use, etc. and includes an Avery cross reference chart. (https://www.worldlabel.com/Templates/free-blank-label-templates-online.htm)

- ✓ **TheBalance.com** has free Resume Templates for Word – (https://www.thebalance.com/free-microsoft-resume-templates-for-word-2063143)

- ✓ **TechTarget.com** created a Disaster Recovery Plan Guide and Template in Word at the following link–

(http://searchdisasterrecovery.techtarget.com/feature/IT-disaster-recovery-DR-plan-template-A-free-download-and-guide)

- ✓ **Workzone.com** Blog offers free resources and the following to-do list templates in Google Sheets.

  - Checklist: http://bit.ly/2z8WN7H

  - Basic To-Do List: http://bit.ly/2zZqOYJ

  - Team To-Do List: http://bit.ly/2jM8i28

Free Software

As mentioned in the previous section, downloading any kind of software is at your own risk. Also, the word "free" can sometimes be deceiving, so be sure to read all of the fine print. Sometimes free software is only offered for a limited amount of time, such as a trial membership. There is also a possibility that the free version of software is a teaser, and the deluxe version has to be purchased in order to obtain access to all of the functionality. You might also have to provide your name and e-mail address in return for access to these software programs.

- ✓ **OpenOffice** has a free version and an upgraded paid version of OpenOffice software, which is compatible with Microsoft Office "Office Suite." (http://www.openoffice.us.com)

  - OpenOffice offers **free templates** for letters, business cards, calendars, etc. (http://www.openoffice.us.com/free-openoffice-templates.php)

✓ **Evernote.com** is available online and via apps to capture information, organize it, and save it for later. There is a free basic version as well as various paid membership options available in an app and online. See how it works at (https://evernote.com/get-started). There is now a new Webclipper feature which will save Websites or you can clip portions of sites to refer back to later. Watch a video on how it works at https://evernote.com/products/webclipper. If you are really adventurous, you can try using an electronic notebook that is compatible with Evernote, DropBox, or OneNote. Pages can be captured through Evernote and/or other apps, and pages are reusable using FriXion pens. You can delete and reuse pages, depending on the type of book you get. Although most include Everlast in the title, they do not last forever, and most pages are only reusable about 10 times. I tried Elfin Everlast Notebook, but was unable to use it because I could not find a compatible app in English. I plan to give one of the other brands a try such as Rocketbook, RUBbook Smart Notebook, or Zohulu Smart Notebook.

✓ **FatPaint.com** – Free graphic design software, page and logo maker

✓ *"20 Great Sites for Free Graphic Design Software and Apps"* from GraphicDesignClasses.net – (http://graphicdesignclasses.net/2012/20-great-sites-for-free-graphic-design-software-and-apps)

✓ **Gimp.org** is a free image editing program. The site includes tutorials on how to use it.

✓ **SumoPaint.com** is an online photo editor and drawing program that allows you to draw your own pictures or edit pictures from other sources. The program is free, and for $9 per year, you can upgrade to a version with no ads that provides you with additional tools to use.

✓ **Color Cop.net** – This is a great program for matching colors in PowerPoint, Web design, and other programs.

Free e-Books, Magazines, and Business News

These Websites contain useful resources for career information and learning new skills in different fields.

- ✓ One of my personal favorite Websites and the newsletter that I subscribe to is **TheMuse.com**. *"Find everything you need to succeed from dream jobs to career advice."* (http://themuse.com)

- ✓ **Free Trade Magazines.com** as mentioned earlier in this book.

- ✓ **Study.com** has an article on *"Free Books - 50 Places to Find Free Books Online"* (https://study.com/articles/Free_Books_-_50_Places_to_Find_Free_Books_Online.html)

- ✓ **BookBoon.com** – Free text books and business books are available for download, if you provide some basic information.

- ✓ **Tradepub.com** – Free "Career Library" with free professional and technical research, white papers, case studies, magazines, and eBooks. (https://mm.tradepub.com)

- ✓ **Business Owners' Idea Café** has free management research, white papers, reports, case studies, magazines, and eBooks. (https://ideacafe.tradepub.com)

- ✓ **Marketing Dive.com** – Offers News, Trends, Jobs, Events, Tools, Press Releases, etc.

- ✓ **Top Ten Reviews.com** offers reviews of products by category (http://www.toptenreviews.com/)

- ✓ **Kiplinger.com** – Personal Finance Advice & Business Forecasts
- ✓ **BPubs.com** – Business Publications Search Engine for articles, publications, reports, papers, etc.

✓ **Bloomsburg Businessweek** – Business news, stock market, and financial advice https://www.bloomberg.com/businessweek

✓ **The Business Journals** by industries and topics (https://www.bizjournals.com)

✓ **The New York Times** – business and financial News https://www.nytimes.com/section/business

✓ **British Broadcasting Corp (BBC)** business news as well as insight and analysis of the United Kingdom and other global markets (http://www.bbc.co.uk/news/business)

✓ **Entrepreneur.com**

✓ **Harvard Business School Weekly Newsletter** (https://hbswk.hbs.edu)

✓ **More Than Money** (MTM) Career articles and tips filed by topic and year (http://morethanmoneycareers.com)

✓ **The Wall Street Journal**: business and financial news (https://www.wsj.com)

✓ **Reuters.com**: Breaking news and videos on business, politics, entertainment, technology and more

✓ **Bloomberg.com** – Business, financial & economic news, stock quotes (https://www.bloomberg.com)

✓ **CNBC.com** – Global business news by region

Travel Tools, Articles, Search Sites, etc.

Some employers have preferred companies that they require you to use when booking travel, so please be sure to familiarize yourself with your company's travel and expense policies. Since rates change frequently, keep in mind that the ticket price may change before you book it. For example, if you get a quoted price for an airline ticket for your boss, and they wait until the next day to give you a decision on whether to buy it, the price may have gone up significantly by the time you book it. Travel prices are often based on demand, and as the plane fills up, the more expensive the seats become. (This is the typical supply and demand rule of any business.)

- ✓ If you are new to booking travel, I highly recommend you read Joan Burge's article on the Office Dynamics International Website, **OfficeDynamics.com**, titled *"How to Plan Business Travel & Business Travel Planning Checklists."* In addition to the article, you can also sign up to receive a 16 page pdf file of Joan's *"Comprehensive Business Travel Planning Guide Vital Resource for Assistants, Business Travelers and Planners"* that provides an extremely thorough step-by-step instruction on how to book travel for an executive. (https://officedynamics.com/how-to-plan-business-travel-business-travel-planning-checklist)

- ✓ **Airport Codes** – (https://www.world-airport-codes.com)

- ✓ **World Travel Guides by US News & World Report.com** – Listed by country and alphabetically by city https://travel.usnews.com/destinations

- ✓ **Country Calling Codes.com** – International

- ✓ **Seat Guru.com** – Seat maps, seat ratings/advice, comfort rating system, and flight shopping. I use this often when booking flights to make sure my boss is not getting assigned a bad seat.

- ✓ **Currency Converter** – (http://www.xe.com)

✓ **Cultural Etiquette** – by country
(http://www.ediplomat.com/np/cultural_etiquette/cultural_etiquette.htm)

✓ **Frommers.com** – Travel guide, trip ideas, news, etc.

✓ **Fodors.com** – Fodor's travel news, guides, travel apps, forums, deals, etc.

✓ **TimeandDate.com** – Current local times and weather around the world as well as calculator, calendar, apps, and articles

✓ **TaxiFareFinder.com** – Easy to use taxi fare estimator that predicts the cost of a taxi (for major US and Canadian cities).

✓ **Tripit.com** – Creates a travel itinerary for you that are either online or mobile friendly (also available in an app and via Concur) The Tripit Pro app is includes additional features such as alerts for cancellations and flight delays, etc. for a monthly fee.

✓ **Passport and Visa Info for US** –
(https://travel.state.gov/content/travel/en/passports.html/passport_1738.html)

✓ **Top Ten Reviews'** *"Best Online Travel Sites of 2018"* –
(www.toptenreviews.com/services/home/best-online-travel-sites)

✓ **Trip Advisor.com** – Reviews and forums about hotels, flights, and vacation rentals, etc.

  ▪ This site is extremely helpful when the majority of the hotels in an area are booked, and there are only a few remaining options. It helps me make the best selection from what is available.

- ✓ **DogFriendly.com** – Travel guide for finding find dog friendly hotels, restaurants, and parks in several cities across the USA and Canada (Books for purchase are now available on Amazon as well)

- ✓ **Kayak.com** – Compares hundreds of sites at once

- ✓ **Expedia com** – Also available in an app.

- ✓ **Orbitz.com** – Also available in an app.

- ✓ **Priceline.com** – Get up to 60% off hotels. Also includes other travel booking options. Also available in an app.

- ✓ **Travelocity.com** – Known best for their mascot the traveling garden gnome and for the phrase "Wander Wisely". You can subscribe to receive additional discounts on hotels.

- ✓ **Hotwire.com** – Discount travel deals featuring reviews from Trip Advisor

- ✓ **TravelZoo.com** – Compare multiple travel sites at once for world-wide trips

- ✓ **BookingBuddy.com** – Compare prices on flights, hotels, cruises, car rentals, etc.

- ✓ **BudgetTravel.com**

Railroads & Busses

Trains are rarely used to book trips at my full-time job. Usually, it is just for short trips between Baltimore and New York City. However, you might be able to use these sites for personal use or rare business occasions.

✓ **RailEurope.com** – Some Americans find this site more user friendly than going directly through local European rail Websites, but keep in mind that the local sites may offer better deals.

✓ **Amtrak.com** – Train and bus tickets for USA and Canada

✓ **Greyhound.com** – Bus tickets for USA, Mexico, and Canada

Hotels

✓ **Trivago.com** – Search over 200 Hotel Booking Sites

✓ Below are the Websites of some commonly used chain hotels:

- **Marriott Hotels & Resorts** (http://marriott.com)

- **Sheraton Hotels & Resorts** (http://starwoodhotels.com)

- **Hilton Hotels & Resorts** (http://www3.hilton.com/en/index.html)

- **The Ritz Carlton** (http://ritzcarlton.com)

- **Choice Hotels**: Quality Inn, Comfort Inn, Sleep, etc. (http://www.choicehotels.com)

- **Hyatt Regency** (https://regency.hyatt.com/en/hyattregency.html)

- **Wyndham** (http://wyndham.com)

- **InterContinental Hotel Group** – Includes several brands, such as InterContinental, Holiday Inn, Crowne Plaza, etc. – (http://ihg.com)

- **HolidayInn Express** (http://hiexpress.com)

- **Howard Johnson Hotels** (http://hojo.com)

Hotel Alternatives & Vacation Rentals

✓ **Booking.com** – Global site that compares hotels, bed and breakfasts, apartments and more

✓ **Airbnb.com** – Their tagline is "Book unique homes and experiences all over the world."

✓ **VacationRentals.com** – Offers deals on homes, beach houses, cabins, and condos, etc.

✓ **VRBO.com** – Homes, condos, and properties in trending areas

Airlines

✓ **One Travel** – Lists toll-free numbers and Websites of airlines in alphabetical order and travel resources (https://www.onetravel.com/travel/airlinenumbers.asp) One Travel appears to have an exhaustive list of Airlines. Below are a few of the ones I use most frequently:

- **American Airlines** – (http://www.aa.com)

- **Delta** – (http://www.delta.com)

- **United** – (http://www.united.com)

- **US Air** – (http://www.usair.com)

- **JetBlue** – (http://www.jetblue.com)

- **AirTran** – (http://www.airtran.com)
- **Southwest Airlines** – (http://www.southwest.com)

- **British Airways** – (http://www.britishairways.com)

Rental Cars

✓ **Hertz Car Rental** (http://www.hertz.com)

✓ **National Car Rental** (http://www.nationalcar.com)

✓ **Enterprise Car Rental**
(https://legacy.enterprise.com/car_rental/home.do)

Restaurant Booking

✓ **Open Table.com**

✓ **Free Bookings.com**

✓ **Restaurant Reservations.com**

✓ **Fodor's Travel Guide: Eat & Drink** –
(https://www.fodors.com/news/category/restaurants)

Career & Personal Development

If you are interested in personal and professional development, I recommend taking advantage of free and low cost webinars and seminars whenever you have the opportunity. Some organizations offer free webinars, such as **ASAP** and **Office Dynamics International**, both of which are mentioned earlier in this book. The following Websites may also be of interest to you, depending on what you are trying to learn. Most of them are free as well!

- ✓ When I need to find an answer or instructions on how to do something, my go-to Websites are **YouTube** and **Google**. It's difficult to remember what life was like before they were invented.☺

- ✓ One of my favorite Websites is **StumbleUpon.com** because it recommends new Websites for you to explore based on your interests.

- ✓ **TED.com** – Ted Talks are on all kinds of topics. "The 25 Most Popular Talks of All" can be found at the following link: (https://www.ted.com/playlists/171/the_most_popular_talks_of_all)

- ✓ **Quick and Dirty Tips.com**: *"Helping You Do Things Better"* – This site offers information on a variety of topics including money, business, career, grammar, etc. (https://www.quickanddirtytips.com)

- ✓ **Microsoft Classes** – For free! Plus templates, tips and tricks, etc. (https://support.office.com/en-us)

- ✓ **Marc and Angel.com** – Marc and Angel Chernoff created their HackLife Website for learning a variety of things including their course on *"Getting Back to Happy."*

  - One of the articles on their site is *"12 Dozen Places to Educate Yourself Online for Free"* To save you doing the math, that's 144 Websites!

(http://www.marcandangel.com/2010/11/15/12-dozen-places-to-self-educate-yourself-online)

- Another helpful article on their site is *"40 Useful Sites to Learn New Skills"* (http://www.marcandangel.com/2010/05/24/top-40-useful-sites-to-learn-new-skills)

✓ **Small Business Administrative Learning Center** classes and resources sponsored by the US Government. (https://www.sba.gov/course)

✓ **Lifehack.org** – Articles on technology, productivity, money, communication, work, and more. The following articles are worth checking out:

- *"25 Killer Sites for Free Online Education"* (https://www.lifehack.org/articles/money/25-killer-sites-for-free-online-education.html)

- *"80 How-To Sites Worth Bookmarking"* (https://www.lifehack.org/articles/featured/80-how-to-sites-worth-bookmarking.html)

✓ **Instructables.com** – Instructions on how to do all kinds of things

✓ **US News & World Report.com** – *"8 Websites for Free Online Learning"* (https://money.usnews.com/money/blogs/my-money/2014/09/23/8-websites-for-free-online-learning)

✓ **Medium.com** – *"The 49 Best Websites and Apps to Learn Something New"* (https://medium.com/the-mission/the-49-best-free-websites-and-apps-to-learn-something-new-abfe69142d4b)

✓ **Answers.com** – *"The Most Trusted Place For Answering Life's Questions"* – Reference sources, answers, etc. (http://answers.com)

✓ **eHow.com** – *"Do-It-Yourself (DIY) and How-To Everything"* (https://www.ehow.com)

✓ **Hubpages.com** – This Website describes itself as, "...a network of sites where people write about their passions!" There is a wide variety of topics that the articles are written about. If you enjoy writing, it is also a way to earn some extra money.

✓ **Infocobuild.com** – Offers videos, documentaries, and lectures from colleges and university all over the world. It also includes free education, games, news, radio, useful Websites, and learning foreign languages.

✓ **PickTheBrain.com** Blog on Motivation and Self Improvement Topics

✓ **Creative Bloq.com** – Inspiration and how-to's on art and design (http://www.creativebloq.com/how-to)

✓ **Learn to Draw** – Step-by-step video tutorials (http://www.DrawingNow.com)

✓ **Netlingo.com** – Largest list of chat terms and internet acronyms and the top 50 texting terms defined (https://www.netlingo.com/top50/popular-text-terms.php)

Meeting Room Set-ups

The following are types of room setups/seating styles to consider when planning meetings and events.

Classroom Style – Forward facing chairs and tables

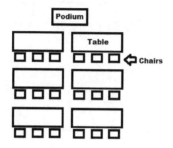

Theatre or Auditorium Style – Chairs only facing forward

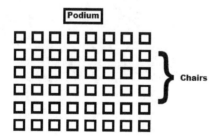

U-Shaped – Tables with chairs around the outside facing forward.

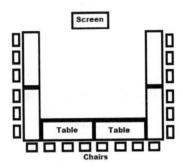

Cocktail or Reception Style – High rounds without chairs or high rounds with chairs around the sides of the room. This allows for mingling. A larger number of people can participate, if the majority is standing.

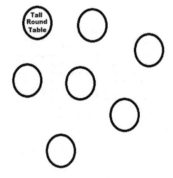

Boardroom or Conference Style – All participants around one large table

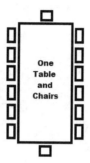

Hollow Square – Tables in a square with chairs around the outside and nothing in the middle. This is good if there are too many people for a Boardroom/Conference Style.)

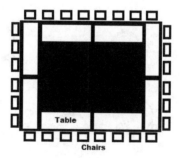

Rounds or Banquet Style – Round tables with chairs all the way around them are often used for dinner or luncheon meetings for large groups. Most often, six, eight, or 10 are at one table, depending on the number of guests.

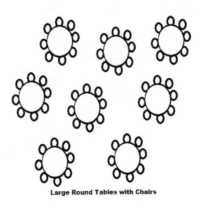

Large Round Tables with Chairs

Half-Rounds or Cabaret Style – Round tables with chairs half-way around them facing forward

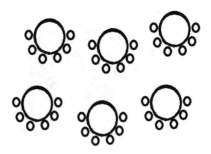

V-Shaped or Chevron Style – With tables on the right and left side of the room in a V angle facing forward.

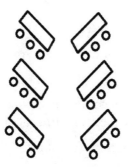

Basic Meeting Planning Checklist

- ☐ Date
- ☐ Time
- ☐ How Many Attendees?
- ☐ Theme, Purpose, and/or Topic of Meeting
- ☐ Agenda?
- ☐ Location (reserve conference room or make arrangements at off-site hotel or location, if needed)
- ☐ Is Catering Required? (Breakfast/Lunch/Snacks? Water or Coffee only?)
- ☐ If so, does the organizer have a preference on type of food? Maybe something to go with the theme?
- ☐ Do any of the attendees have food allergies or dietary restrictions to keep in mind when ordering? (Vegan, Kosher, Peanut Allergies, etc.)
- ☐ How should the room be set-up?
    - ☐ Is a lectern required for the speaker?
    - ☐ Are tables required? (They usually will if laptops will be used and/or people will be eating.)
- ☐ Audio/Visual Requirements
- ☐ Conference Call
- ☐ Webinar/Go-To-Meeting
- ☐ Video Conference
- ☐ Microphone
- ☐ Speakers for pc for playing video/audio clips
- ☐ Flip Charts/Markers?
- ☐ Are special supplies required? Post-its? Pens? Pads?
- ☐ Handouts/Copies required for participants?
- ☐ Do notebooks/viewbinders, etc. need to be ordered?

"Mom Bag" Checklist for Seminars/Large Meetings

If you are coordinating a big meeting or off-site seminar/conference, it is a good idea to have a "Mom Bag" with some basic supplies and items for first-aid or things you may need for yourself or participants in case of unforeseen emergencies. Some items may include the following:

- [ ] Pens and notepads
- [ ] Post-it Notes
- [ ] Tylenol and/or Advil
- [ ] Sewing Kit / Safety Pins
- [ ] Phone Charger
- [ ] Computer Charger
- [ ] Scissors
- [ ] Tape / Paper Clips / Stapler
- [ ] Masking Tape (to tape flip chart paper to walls in case you don't have post-it paper)
- [ ] Packing Tape
- [ ] Duct Tape (to cover up plugs/wires for safety)
- [ ] Bandages
- [ ] Hand sanitizer
- [ ] Laser Pointer
- [ ] Remote to advance slides ("clicker")
- [ ] AA and AAA batteries
- [ ] Anti-acids / Pepto-Bismol / Imodium
- [ ] Cough Drops / Cold or Sinus Meds
- [ ] Mints / Gum
- [ ] Extra flip chart and/or white board markers
- [ ] Original of Handouts, in case extra copies are needed

New Employee Setup Checklist

☐ Submit requests to IT/HelpDesk for laptop/pc equipment, phone setup, and cell phone request, etc. as applicable

☐ Review all safety procedures, evacuation routes, and shelter in place information

☐ Give them snow emergency plan/phone number, if applicable

☐ Orient them to building or campus

☐ Email links to important company Intranet and/or SharePoint sites

☐ Provide organizational charts, if applicable

☐ Cafeteria menu and/or list of local restaurants

☐ Show them supply cabinet(s) and provide them with some basic supplies such as:

　☐ Pens / Pencils

　☐ Highlighter

　☐ Notepad

　☐ Stapler / Staple Remover / Staples

　☐ Tape & Dispenser

　☐ Scissors

　☐ Trash Can & Recycling Bin

　☐ Paper Clips

　☐ Calendar

　☐ Ruler

☐ Create Mailbox

Basic Travel Checklist

Be sure to talk with your boss first to find out their preferences when traveling, i.e. isle or window seat, etc. It is also important to familiarize yourself with your company's travel and expense policies. If you are using Concur or a similar program, there is a profile for each traveler already established with their personal preferences as well as their frequent flyer and hotel loyalty program numbers.

☐ Arrival/Departure dates and times. Remember that some trips have multiple stops/legs

☐ Arrival/Departure destinations (Make sure you have the correct airport codes as several destinations have more than one airport.)

☐ Arrival/Departure Transportation

☐ Will they be driving to the airport or do they need an Uber, Lift, Taxi, or Sedan service to take them?

☐ Will they need a rental car, transportation arrangements, or is someone picking them up or meeting them at the airport when they arrive?

☐ How do they plan to return to the airport and how will they get home once they land?

☐ Create a travel folder for each trip that includes the following at a minimum. (It is better to provide too much information than not enough. They can always take out what they do not want to take on the trip with them later.)

☐ Itinerary – Print out the confirmation itinerary from booking the trip. Some executives prefer a step-by-step itinerary typed up for them with every single detail from the time they leave their home until the time they return home including meetings, dinners, etc. (Remember – The less your executive has to worry about the logistics/details, the more time they have to concentrate on more important issues.)

  o Some bosses will ask you to e-mail a copy of their itinerary to a spouse or family member.

☐ Transportation information and directions (unless they prefer to use their phone, Google Maps, etc.)

☐ Information on hotel. (I usually print out the facts or "about us" page of their Website.)

☐ Information about the weather while they are there, so they will know how to pack.

☐ Presentation slides (hard copy and on USB drive)

☐ Any executive reports or background information they need on customers or clients they may be meeting while they are there.

☐ Safety information and/or emergency contact info in case they need it.

☐ Extra copy of their passport and visa, if they are traveling overseas.

☐ Cultural information and some background on the location, if they have never traveled to that destination before.

Disclosure Statement

IMPORTANT NOTICE:

DISCLAIMER AND LEGAL NOTICES:

About the Author

Penney D. Simmons, CAP has over 30 years of experience in the administrative field. Penney started her own company, Professional Office Plus LLC, in March 2011. She obtained her certification as a Certified Administrative Professional (CAP) through International Association of Administrative Professionals (IAAP) in 2003. Penney graduated Magna Cum Laude from Strayer University earning a Bachelor's degree in Business Administration with a concentration in Business Management. Penney is also a member of various professional organizations.

ISBN-10: 1983913936
ISBN-13: 9781983913938

Professional Office Plus LLC
1213 Liberty Road
Suite #191
Eldersburg, MD 21784
professionalofficeplus@gmail.com
www.bestexecutiveassistant.com

CPSIA information can be obtained
at www.ICGtesting.com
Printed in the USA
LVHW080258100120
643210LV00015B/398/P

9 781983 913